CONTENTS

Cover Picture: Denver.
Title Page: Corn harvesting, Four Gotes

DENVER

Front cover illustration

Earlier attempts to drain the fens were as nothing compared to the undertaking by the Dutchman, Cornelius Vermuyden, before and after the Civil War on behalf of the Duke of Bedford and his Company of Adventurers, who were to share 95,100 acres of drained land for financing the scheme. The winding rivers that could never carry the water were relieved by channels named the New and Old Bedford rivers, cut from Earith in Cambridgeshire to Denver in Norfolk 22 miles away, supplemented by the Fortyfoot, Twentyfoot and Sixteenfoot Drains flowing into the Middle Level Drain at St. German's for lifting into the Great Ouse seven miles from The Wash. The expanse of washland between the two Bedford rivers is there to hold the surplus water during the wet season. Countless windmills once lifted the water from fen level and the flow to the sea is governed by great sluices at St. German's and Denver.

The original Denver Sluice lasted until 1713, when it collapsed. It was replaced only after 35 years of wrangling between navigators who were against building it and the drainers who wanted it rebuilt. Meanwhile the fens reverted to their wet state, although memories of the way many of its inhabitants had lived off the waters had faded. The drainers won and the second sluice is seen here on July 31st, 1891 with the figures carefully arranged and ordered still for the photographer. Vermuyden, who had become naturalised and been knighted before coming to the fens, had envisaged a further channel skirting the fens on the eastern side, but this was thwarted by lack of funds. The greatest tribute to his planning was paid to him when his plan was implemented after ten years of preparation and ten more of construction and the new channel opened in 1964.

(Central Divisional Library, King's Lynn; Taylor Slide Collection)

ACKNOWLEDGEMENTS

I am indebted to so many unidentified brief encounters in these villages, for those who could offer little direct information were pleased to point me in the right direction. I am, as always, indebted to the archives put at my disposal and the patient help given by the compilers. In particular I thank Michael Petty and his staff at the Cambridgeshire Collection, David Rayner of the District Library in Wisbech, Jane Lineham and Tony Lake of the Central Divisional Library, King's Lynn and David Devonish, curator, and Bill Weston of the Wisbech and Fenland Museum. The indispensable long memories and local knowledge on which I have relied belong to the following: Doris Wheatley of Swavesey, Alec Badcock of Cottenham, Hilda Hatley, Keith Hinde and Muriel Seekings of Waterbeach, John Webb of Lode, Albert Fleet, Gwynneth Jeffrey and Vernon Place of Isleham, Henry Barnes of Wicken, Iliffe Norfolk and Roger Brew of Wilburton, Chris Jakes of Prickwillow, Mrs. P.M. Trevers, Elsie Crane, Margaret Missin and Mrs. D. Adams of Little Downham, Mrs. T. Bourne of Coveney, Sheila Collins of Witchford, Mrs. D.A. Yarrow of Wentworth, Alf Sharpe of Witcham, Bill Read and Bill Readhead of Sutton, Wilf Kilby and Mrs. B. Faux of Mepal, Mrs. K. Moat of Manea, Miss B.A. Double of Doddington, Hilda Andrews of Outwell, Frank Quince of Emneth, Brian Payne of Cambridge and Guyhirn, Hugh Cave — Mr. Thorney himself — Albert Gee and J.L. Gregory of Thorney, Henry Shippey and Mr. and Mrs. Pritchard of Newton, Eric Trundle and Neville Carter of Tydd St. Giles, Mr. and Mrs. G. Reynolds, Mr. and Mrs. Powley and Jack Burlington of Terrington St. John, Kathleen Lack and Terry and Maureen Harness of Tilney St. Lawrence and Dr. A.W. Greer of Walpole Highway for photographs and information on that and the neighbouring villages and for taking the trouble to bring these to me. It was a great pleasure to meet all these people and to share their memories. Finally I am grateful for the encouragement and support of Steve Benz of S.B. Publications.

THE AUTHOR

Anthony Day is a professional landscape painter who also writes. He studied art at the Cambridge School of Art from 1948 to 1952 and at Reading University from 1954 to 1955, thereafter specialising in painting the fen country and its towns, selling his work through dealers in London and East Anglia and mixed exhibitions such as the Royal Academy and the Royal Society of British Artists.

For fourteen years he was art critic to the 'Cambridge Evening News' but he is now principally interested in writing about country matters and local history. Recent articles by him have been published in 'The Countryman' and 'Cambridgeshire Life'. He has assembled a huge archive of photographs of his native village of Wicken which he has used in books, exhibitions and slide-shows and took part in the important 'Fen Archive' exhibition at the Cambridge Darkroom gallery in 1986, the catalogue of which is now a collectors' item.

INTRODUCTION

They lie calmer than any sea from the fringes of Cambridge into marshland to The Wash, far into Norfolk and Lincolnshire, more often than not emptier of life than when they were under water. The fields of the fens and marshland today are forbidden places for all but the few who till them, flowerless, in all shades of unbroken green in summer — corn green, sugarbeet, carrot, celery, dark potato and pale lettuce green, and where you spot the land returning to its old waterlogged state you come across a polythene ocean forcing the salad plants along.

Gone are the hoeing and harvesting gangs, the women and boys crawling along the land singling sugarbeet or heads-down sowing or gathering potatoes. The Norfolk bonnets have long since been set aside or given to the folk museums. There are no autumn stacks to catch the setting sun. As a fenman and painter I love the space around me but I miss the warm features I found into the 1960s. The four tidy stacks I put into a painting of 1964 happened to be the last built by that farmer who then acquired a combine harvester. Now the views are accented by serried ranks of new trees, by the lone tractor trailing its venomous wings, the combines moving like giant snails, the sugarbeet harvester tumbling its roots into the empty trailer alongside and the potato lifter sheltering its crew of sorters behind heavy cloths. Yet the light and the skies — those huge skies — are the same — or, should I say, never the same from one day to the next where the unobstructed horizon is my birthright.

I offer here glimpses of life not so very long ago in the villages of fen and marshland, situated above the level, built there to manage the land around. Those I interviewed there had much the same story to tell of a lost way of life, set against the gains. These gains are indisputable. Improved sanitation and electricity were blessings when they came to these isolated communities but the car that began as a novelty and luxury too soon became a necessity to get to work. In such a short space of time, after hundreds of years of little change these villages lost their innate character and community spirit. The local speech telling us how people spoke hundreds of years ago is giving way to outside influences. Such was unthinkable a few decades ago.

The twentieth century was a long time altering life there, but it has made up for lost time since the 1960s. Two world wars made little difference. Those lucky enough to survive came home confirmed in their belief in the old values. The industrial revolution did nothing to alter things. The coming of the railways with all those little village stations were never there to tempt people away for long and buses were merely quicker than bikes. The steam age only revolutionised fen drainage and if the petrol and paraffin engines installed by farmers to grind their own corn into meal deprived the miller of the work, he too was glad to instal one to drive his mill on windless days. Tractors put nobody out of work. I was farming with horses until 1938 and as tractors replaced horses the horsekeepers learned to drive them and become good mechanics. Then came the mechanical harvesters long after they had been introduced abroad; chemicals replaced manpower and all those school chums of mine who had been brought up to work on the land like their forebears — and could hardly wait to get there — had to seek work elsewhere. They cycled out until it was imperitive to own a car and the villages were emptier by day than they had ever been. The rush to live in the country began, the more isolated the better, and, indeed, newcomers have done wonders for preservation where villagers were too ready to remove the old for the new; but they can do little to keep the schools and the shops open or to keep the communities truly alive.

These photographs outline the end of an era, of hard work and soft celebration. They evoke the sounds and smells of the countryside that we who were born to them continue to miss. They show some of the happy neglect that made village life what it was. Modern devices force people to compete for tidiness; to let a hedge have its way or leave a fruit tree unpruned is unthinkable. Legions of leylandii conifers have chilled the vistas and gardens are kept flat and cold. Feeling for the richness of nature is disappearing fast while people pay tribute to conservation. The elder bush is treated as a weed and tidy rows of bedding plants are preferred to glorious profusion. Villages have caught the trend and have discarded so much of what they were given. The garden centres have a lot to answer for. I hope this book will underline these views.

Anthony Day
Wicken

SWAVESEY

This was where the fens began for many Cambridge people attracted by skating of the highest standard on Mare Fen. It was less easy to travel the ten miles in 1891 and 1895 than in 1929 when the amateur skating championship of Great Britain was raced here. The professional variation was staged in 1887 and 1895, a vintage year. Swavesey is largely Victorian and there are many plain cottages, but it has some fine earlier houses and a beautiful church. This scene near Swan Pond in the late 1890s was devastated by fire in 1913. We are looking towards Church End along the road to Over and Willingham with The Chequers public house on the right, then administered by Mrs. Lucy Mitham, and the strangely named Swan with Two Necks opposite the pond on the left, where Jonas Thorp was mine host and where his wife, Elizabeth, succeeded him. This escaped the fire and is known today as The Merchant House. Floods sometimes rose to this level and the cottages are banked against them. The banks are still there, ornately retained today.

(Cambridgeshire Collection)

SWAVESEY

This is the scene after the fire of March 3rd, 1913. It began in Taylor's Lane and spread to Church End and although the pond was at hand the fire engines could not halt the flames before they devoured those cottages of wattle and daub and thatch. 66 people were made homeless, many of them uninsured. Those who were soon had their claims settled to the extent of £600, but a fund was launched to help the others. This accrued so rapidly that a provision was made to build homes for the elderly on the site opposite the ruined cottages with the surplus total. The outcome was Frere House offering three units for single occupants or couples. Sightseers gorged on the scene of this fire. They arrived in droves on the following Sunday, March 9th. The Bishop of Ely gave thanks in the church that no lives were lost. The pond is now well kept in this most attractive part of Swavesey.
(Cambridgeshire Collection)

2

Denmark Road, Cottenham

COTTENHAM

The road from Cambridge and Histon winds and undulates through this long village on the edge of the fens, which today has a population around five thousand. The prettiest corner of the village is near the church where the road turns and dips to fen level on its way to Wilburton. The ornate tower of All Saints Church looks almost Muscovian across the open fen. Cottenham was once the seat of the Pepys family and it was Katherine Pepys who paid for the rebuilding of the church steeple after its destruction by storm in 1617. The village is older than it looks, having suffered from fires between 1676 and 1849, incendiarists being to blame. If cows were never as sacred here as in India they seemed to have a great freedom to roam the streets. The ladies mingle unflinchingly here in Denmark Road, never lifting their skirts off the ground while decency prevailed. The cottage on the left is intact, but the one farther along has lost its charm and character to a corrugated iron roof.

(Cambridgeshire Collection)

3

COTTENHAM

The village was once renowned for its cheese-making and later for its fruit and flower-growing on a grand scale, which employed the majority of its native population. It once had the largest fruit-growing acreage of any village in Cambridgeshire, but the decline that began seriously in the 1950s has left Cottenham with only a few families active in the business. There were many part-time growers, but they had all gone by the 1960s, giving way to heavy importations of fruit. Here one of them, Ed Badcock, who lived in Little End that has now become New Road, who grew his produce in Beach Road, pauses with his wife after making deliveries from door to door during the height of the strawberry season after the First World War. Carriers once arrived here daily to convey fruit to large towns.

(Cambridgeshire Collection)

4

COTTENHAM

Here, at 256 High Street, Cottenham, in the mid-1920s, is the shop of wheelwright and undertaker E.H. Haird and the garage of A.V. Haird with appropriate forms of transport in front. The motorcycle on the left belonged to Mr. Forest Adamson and the combination on the right, which had been adapted to serve as a milk-float, to Mr. Fred Ward of Histon. The assembled company are, left to right: Jack Diddell, George Haird, the wheelwright and undertaker, Victor Haird the garage proprietor, Thomas Male, a gardener, Mr. Kimpton, retired, Mr. Smith a hirer of threshing tackle, John Hart of Hart's Foundry here, Ernest Scott, another gardener and Mr. Carter who was generally unemployed like so few hereabouts at this time. Today the site is Eastland's Garage incorporating the house behind which is now numbered 262.

(Cambridgeshire Collection)

WILLINGHAM

Linked to Cottenham by three miles of narrow road through Rampton, Willingham is a compact village for its size. The population at the time of this photograph in the 1890s was above 1,600. The village was known for its fruit-growing from the 16th century, but this became large-scale only after 1875. There were 750 acres of orchards by the 1930s, but our age has decimated them. These were above fen level. The Conqueror's route to Ely passed near Willingham and the barely conspicuous earthwork, Belsar's Hill, might have been the base for his attacks on Hereward. The scene here in Church Street shows cottages now gone. Wilfred Day's bakery later occupied the unthatched cottage showing against the church and today another bakery is installed on the corner of Church Lane. St. Mary's and All Saints Church was formerly St. Matthew's, changing in the early 18th century to All Saints and changing again in 1763. The public house on the right was The Windmill until it changed much later to the more appropriate Ringers' Rest.
(Cambridgeshire Collection)

WILLINGHAM

Growing osiers for the purpose of basket making was once common in the fens. The baskets made necessarily lightweight containers for harvesting potatoes and fruit and had many domestic uses. The wetlands were ideal for growing the willows which were cut back to sprout the thin stems required. These were soaked overnight and stripped, mainly by women and children eager to supplement their income during a harvesting season beginning in April and lasting but a month. The stems were drawn through claves and bundled into small, medium and long lengths and this scene of activity is at Cole's Yard, Willingham, in the 1890s. The peelers would get twopence or twopence-halfpenny a bundle for this work. It was one of many casual jobs open to them during the year; others, particularly in this village, were fruit gathering, potato picking and helping with the corn harvest. While the women had their children beside them there was no problem of supervision at home. Until recent times osiers were also used for weaving huge mattresses to be floated down rivers and sunk under stones for temporary dams.

(Cambridgeshire Collection)

EARITH

The river Ouse, having meandered through the green meadows of Huntingdonshire, steers off in three directions at Earith. A sluice controls the level in the Old Bedford river but the parallel New Bedford is tidal and, indeed The Wash tide can be seen rolling in daily while diminishing in effect as it meets the Ouse. Porpoises sometimes follow it in and become stranded on the broad step of the bank. Ahead the Ouse meets Hermitage Lock, beyond which it becomes the Old West river until it joins the Cam at the Fish and Duck inn beyond Stretham and becomes the Great Ouse. Earith is a long, typically plain fen village — plainer than this view from early this century showing cottages now replaced. Travelling through into Needingworth you might be forgiven for thinking you were in Earith again, so alike are they in shape and character.

(Cambridgeshire Collection)

EARITH

Learning to skate was once but a short move away from learning to walk in the fen country. In frozen midwinter there was little a farm worker could do to earn his bread and the farmer would be more than happy to lay him off without pay. There was no better way to allay fears of starvation than skating in fierce competition, re-shaping those ploughman's legs to achieve almost balletic grace. This transformation had to be seen to be believed. Leisurely skating, such as we see here on Bury Fen, Earith, with Bluntisham church enchanting the distance, was also a delight. This fen was deliberately flooded from the river in anticipation of frosts enough to permit championship skating and Bury Fen was the rink that succeeded those at Swavesey and Lingay Fen near Cambridge. The amateur championships of Great Britain were held here in 1947 and several years thereafter. This quiet scene is from the 1930s.
(Cambridgeshire Collection; D.G. Reid)

9

WATERBEACH

Perhaps the people of Cambridge glimpsed the worst aspects of fen life here, before travelling farther out to Swavesey. Here lived as curate from 1767 to 1770 the renowned archivist and historian, William Cole, who left testimony to the wet state of land owned by him here at this time. Living in a damp, leaky vicarage, long since replaced, Cole owned farmland to supplement his meagre income, but he was soon describing how he and other farmers were ever apt to grow poorer on account of the floods. 'Not being a water-rat,' Cole soon left for higher ground a little nearer Cambridge. Some very old cottages stood the strain of flooding very well, including one in Salmon Lane — named after the family living in it — now called Way Lane. Built in 1650, it was at last demolished in 1960. Its last occupant, Mr. Rumble, now lives in a bungalow on the site. About 1,300 lived in drier conditions here at the time of this photograph, c.1910, and this beach above the waters has become a much favoured village that owes much to the central green on the right.

(Cambridgeshire Collection)

LODE

Reached by the B1102 off the A45 Cambridge to Newmarket route, Lode was part of Bottisham until November 1894. Even now the road between remains Lode Rode rather than Bottisham Road, Lode. It was the commercial part using Bottisham Lode, the river Cam and later the railway station on the Cambridge-Mildenhall line, which closed in 1962. The Lode half has the greater charm, with many thatched cottages that survived a plague of fires here last century. Ten cottages and William Webb's carpentry workshop were burned down in June 1853 and poor Webb, the owner of two of the cottages fully insured, was arrested on suspicion of arson. His palpable innocence was soon proved and the Webb family trade continues in Lode today. This view along the High Street in 1908 shows three thatched survivors, but only one remains. The brick cottages in the middle contain the post office now, while the shop at the end was owned by Horace Lee. The thatched cottage beyond is now owned by the National Trust. The school beyond was pulled down and there is a new house on the site, yet the school outbuildings were listed and retained. The house jutting out at the end has been replaced. Opposite is the Three Horseshoes public house but the cottage on the left came down in 1913.

(Cambridgeshire Collection)

LODE

Success came to these cricketing juniors in 1935. They are the Lode Junior Cricket team who won the under-eleven schoolboys cup in that Silver Jubilee Year. They are, left to right, back row: Ron Wright, Dennis Gates, Arthur Perry, Charlie Smith, Walter Purr, Gilbert Wright, Ken Brand and George Perry. Front: John Hatley, Len Fry, Ken Wright, Charlie March, and Reg Marsh. Lode owes much to the Broughton family and the thatched village hall was given in memory of Urban Broughton MP who having been given a peerage died before he could receive it. It was conferred on his son who became Lord Fairhaven, living in the grand Anglesey Abbey in beautiful grounds nearby, which is now owned by the National Trust and is open to the public.

(Cambridgeshire Collection)

SWAFFHAM BULBECK

Still skirting the fens we come to Swaffham Bulbeck a mile from Lode, endowed with attractive cottages, dignified farmhouses and various buildings converted for domestic use. The 14th century church of St. Mary is the crowning feature, well-lit with quaint creatures carved on arm-rests and the poppyheads, including mermaids, griffins and fish with feet and animal heads. Its walls of clunch, quarried nearby, have withstood the years well and clunch cottages survive here too. This view along the High Street, c.1910, with the chancel of the church just showing on the far right shows changes today but has largely kept its character. William Watson was the shoemaker who also owned the shop and post office and next to his premises is the Ivy Green public house when its tenant was Walter Levitt, now a private house shorn of its ivy. The next house is beautifully maintained along with its setting of very English trees and shrubs. Much has changed beyond, but the cottages at the very end remain while the building on the right has gone. Commercial End is part of the village, where goods once arrived by Swaffham Lode and where now almost every building has been turned into a desirable residence.

(Cambridgeshire Collection; Frederick Gillson)

13

VIEW OF VILLAGE   SWAFFHAM PRIOR

SWAFFHAM PRIOR

Half a mile on is Swaffham Prior, which has two churches in one churchyard and two windmills, well restored, on one hill. These were the hamlets of Swoet, one belonging afterwards to the Bulbeck family, the other to the Prior. The village sits on solid chalk, or clunch, well above its fens and is blessed with fine houses, cosy cottages and sloping gardens. Peace reigns where the bypass carries the traffic. St. Mary's of Norman origin is the parish church, once struck by lightning after which its steeple was removed. The tower has been well reconstructed and a small aluminium spire added which tends to sound off when it heats up and cools down. The church of St. Cyriac and his mother Julitta, after falling into ruin and having an 18th century nave built on to its 15th century tower in 1806, has, since 1972, been maintained by the Redundant Churches Fund to be used for services, concerts and exhibitions to further the cause of maintenance. This view along Lower End towards Reach from about 1910 is quite recognisable today. The cottage on the right has gone but the next building survives much altered, as does the tiny cottage beyond it. Some of the far cottages remain, but the fine farmhouse left has gone, leaving the clunch wall intact.

(Cambridgeshire Collection)

14

REACH

The pre-Roman Devil's Dyke begins seven miles away at Woodditton and ends here at what was once a vital port receiving ships from abroad. The dyke once continued down to the fen, dividing Reach between Swaffham Prior a mile away, which had by far the greater part, and Burwell, which is nearer two miles away by the winding road, but it was levelled to unite this small village surrounding a green as a separate parish. The church in this view from c.1910 was built in 1860 on the site of the Chapel of St. Etheldreda, a drawing of which dated Rogation Sunday 1768 shows it already in ruins. A small part of it remains. The cottage this side of the church was The Ship public house which became a private house, but it had been unoccupied for some time before being demolished in the 1960s. The school behind it has long been closed but the building is now the Reach Village Centre.
(Cambridgeshire Collection)

REACH

King John granted an annual fair to Reach to be held on Rogation Monday and the traditional opening of it by the mayor of Cambridge continues today, although the date has been shifted to coincide with Spring bank holiday. The mayor arrives as here early this century with his macebearer and train, casting newly-minted coins to the crowd and in my day between the wars we children almost fought to gather them up. The clerk reads the proclamation, warning all intending wrongdoers to behave, the mayor opens the fair on the green, takes the first ride on the roundabouts or makes a show of joining in and the party sit for lunch in the village centre that was formerly the schoolroom before returning. Soon after this the mayor's year of office ends.
(Cambridgeshire Collection)

BURWELL

Along its two-mile length the face of this fen-edge village has changed little since this photograph was taken early this century, although the population has more than doubled to 4,830 in 1990. Apart from the strewn road, the fashions and the absence of cars this could be the scene today. Anne Fuller kept the Five Bells public house on the left, where stands surely the tallest man in Burwell. The village's many recent developments are well concealed from the main street. The splendid 15th century church has a flint exterior with a clunch interior. At a time when the country was plagued with robber barons King Stephen, during his long war with Queen Matilda, had a castle built here. The plunderer hereabouts, who even robbed the churches ignored by others of his kind, was Sir Geoffrey de Magnaville (or Mandeville) who was at last slain by an arrow as he stormed this castle. It has all gone now and the parish council now owns the site and allow public access.

(Cambridgeshire Collection)

BURWELL

There were uprisings in Burwell in 1851 after land set aside for the poor was sold to settle arrears of taxes. However, the Reverend J.J. Baines of Bottisham bought the land for £90 and gave it back to the parish, a fine example of matching money to beliefs. Poor management followed, inducing former tenants to reclaim the land and it took the Metropolitan Police and the military to settle the dispute, happily without bloodshed. Among the rioters had been some whose habit was to dig peat, or turf, for the season between March and August and idle and drink away their time in between while the money lasted. The turf industry here employed as many as three hundred men, women and boys up to the turn of the century, but demand declined after that — apart from an upsurge during the First World War. Diggers, as shown here c.1910, worked to a neat plan, taking the turves out wet, stacking them by the trench to dry for at least six weeks then putting them into stacks inside or out or straight on to boats or barges for transportation to Cambridge or Lynn.

(Cambridgeshire Collection; Frederick Gillson)

18

111514. Isleham Church before the tower fell in 1862. From an Old Engraving

ISLEHAM

Seven miles northwards from Burwell, Isleham was another fen-edge village dependent on both turf-digging and crops from the fens spreading away on three sides. Long ago it was spelt Yselham but the pronunciation was the same. It had dire flooding problems below well into this century, while earlier its badly drained fens became unmanageable for months, a not unfamiliar story in the fens. From that level its 14th century church of St. Andrew stands high and proud, but it once had its problems. Here we see it celebrated by an engraver not long before the tower collapsed in 1862 and although it was never restored to its original design the church remains a fine example of the period.

(Cambridgeshire Collection)

ISLEHAM

Elizabeth Brown living nearby heard the collosal roar of tumbling masonry, came out to see an impenetrable cloud of dust and wondered how many men had been killed and how to tend the wounded. But here was the proof of miracles. Dedicated in 1331, the church replaced an earlier one on the site, of which traces remain in the stonework of the north-east corner of the nave and in the 13th century T-tracery in the north chapel. For a time it seemed that this church too would have to be replaced but on July 22nd 1862 at about half-past five in the evening it was the tower alone, while undergoing restoration, that fell. The workmen had just retreated to The Griffin public house for hard earned refreshment. One of them had earlier seen a mullion fall and gave warning of imminent catastrophe, so they retired to think about it and were saved. A small Benedictine priory was built in Isleham between 1080 and 1090. It was abandoned by monks from 1254 and became a barn but through the Department of Environment and the inspiration of the Reverend J.B. Goodchild it was restored and for the first time for 700 years evensong was conducted there in July 1952.

(Cambridgeshire Collection)

ISLEHAM

If from the foregoing it appears that religion was central to life in Isleham perhaps the following anecdote will confirm it: in 1849 an Isleham man agreed to submit to chloroform for the removal of his damaged finger. While apparently unconcious and feeling no pain he sang a hymn all the way through the·operation, which was wholly successful. Isleham has several disused lime quarries from which the excavated blocks of clunch were used for building and the chippings for processing into lime. Kilns used for this are preserved at Limestone Close, with descriptions of the method. Houses were built in some abandoned pits and such are shown here c.1930 where, nearby, were the Maid's Head public house run by Jack and Rose Harvey with a grocery and sweetshop attached and another grocery and meat shop run by Mrs. Cooke. Here on a bright day brightened further by the white walls stand Ambrose Becket, who was born in the cottage on the right, and Miss Austin, whose home was also here. Only one of these clunch cottages remain, plus a few clunch walls, but new cottages replaced them. The adjacent pit is being prepared for homes for the elderly, but the climb might prove daunting.

(Cambridgeshire Collection; D.G. Reid)

21

WICKEN

Wicken men rose as fiercely as any against the drainage of the fens and they won a concession. Long dependent on fish, fowl, turves, reed and sedge they were placated when an expanse of wild fen was left but partly drained for their use and this today is the famous Wicken Fen administered by the National Trust. The system for harvesting sedge created a haven for fen plants and insects second to none in the region. Its first appointed keeper was Bill Barnes (1878-1968) who came from Wisbech. Bill is seen here in 1935 in a photograph commemorating his first 21 years in the job. The boat on the left for transporting sedge and reeds was Bill's own, made of oak for £32 by Dunnatt's of Burwell. About the same time he bought the boat he is standing in but the National Trust bought it off him and returned it for his own use. We see here on Wicken Lode where the turf boats arrived at the storage sheds. A boatload of turf is moored behind and the turf shed on the right was the last to be built in Wicken, where digging ended in 1939. Bill was succeeded as keeper by his sons Henry and Wilfred. A warden is now in charge.

(Author's Collection)

WICKEN

Once surrounded on three sides by water, Wicken is a promontory seven miles from Burwell by road but only two miles away by footpath across the fen. The road into the village from Newmarket, Fordham and Soham stopped at the river Cam until 1928 when a permanent bridge was built there and another over the Old West river nearer Stretham taking the route across Stretham Mere. Previously the only way through was via the Upware ferry into droves to Waterbeach or through the little settlement of Padney on to the Ely road. Alas for what this did for the traffic flow through Wicken today! Speed is the essence for most of the drivers and few, for good or bad, are likely to stop at the village hostelry, the Maid's Head. Ale has been served there since 1579, but the original was burned down on July 25, 1983. We see it here in 1892 when Ann Bowet Kettle was the licensee. She was the widow of James who had also been the wheelwright using the adjoining sheds, allowing the wood to season on the village green. The Kettle family also kept a shop in the mill house. The Maid's Head today is a remarkable facsimile of the original.

(Birmingham Library Services; P.J. Deakin)

WICKEN

The governmental axe fell on Wicken school in 1992, following the familiar complaint that not enough children attended out of a population of below 700 to justify its continuation. The parents of those attending disagreed and campaigned vigorously against closure and the loss of yet another village amenity, but without ultimate success. So ended the provision begun by Sarah Rayner of Wicken Hall, who gave Wicken its first school in 1831. Percy John Walling, appointed headmaster in 1906, was soon campaigning for a new building and he won this in 1908. Mr. Walling taught, with his wife, until 1946 and is remembered with affection and gratitude. This is Mrs. Walling's classroom in 1931. Reading left to right, the three girls in the nearest desk are Beatrice Bird, Joyce Earl and Rhoda Hawes. Behind them, strictly left to right are: Peter Crow, Stuart Canham, Geoffrey Canham, George Sampher, Jackie Grummet, George Bird, Cecil Bailey, Roy Pamment, Wilfred Barnes, Basil Gandy and Douglas Clements. Next row: Jean MacLaren, Molly Barnes, Joan Gandy, Winifred Barber, Peggy Wright, Sylvia Aworth, Ruby Samms, Florence Wright, Bertha Samms, Edith Delph, Gladys Griggs, Sylvia Redit and Dorothy Griggs. Along the desks on the left: Jessica Clay, Crystal Harding, George Bullman, Phyllis Houghton, Fred Collins, Eric Griggs and Charles Collins.
(Author's Collection)

UPWARE

Central to the drainage systems of the area were two great pumping stations at Upware, standing very close together, lifting the water up to the Cam. The shell of the Burwell engine house at the head of Commissioners Drain, which runs parallel with Burwell Lode, still stands but its function has ceased. Its first steam engine was installed in 1821 and it was replaced by a gas engine in 1895, which was destroyed by fire in 1913. An auxillary paraffin burner kept the pumps going a long time. The first Swaffham engine at the head of Swaffham Main Drain was also installed in 1821 but a new building and a magnificent beam engine replaced it in 1850. A diesel engine succeeded this in 1927, installed in an adjoining shed that still stands, although the main engine with the engine house came down in 1939. This view of the Swaffham engine in 1925 includes the bridge and lock at Burwell Lode and the Anchor public house, which had also been a cafe. The Burwell engine stands behind the fence on the left. Upware, within the parish of Wicken, is a tiny hamlet but it once had its own school which is now a field study centre.
(Cambridgeshire Collection)

UPWARE

The Stevens family were synonymous with fen drainage during the age of steam pumps. The patriarch was William who was engineer at the Little Downham engine by the New Bedford river until he was appointed Superintendent of Drainage to the Waterbeach and Swaffham Commissioners and engineer at the Swaffham engine, Upware. His son Arthur succeeded him, a little against the odds since William guarded his knowledge from any assistant, including Arthur. Eventually he learnt enough to become engineer but not to become superintendent. He and his family of three daughters and a son lived in Ivy Cottage near the engine where, going by the dedicated camera of his daughter Rosa in the 1920s, they lived an idyllic life. Here Rosa the silent spinster captures her parents at ease, Arthur reading his paper, Louisa mending socks. She was nurse and midwife to the fen dwellers on call night and day, ready to trudge miles through sludge, dust or snow sooner than any doctor. Once the diesel engine had been installed Arthur lost heart for his role and soon retired, firstly to Soham then to Wicken where he tended his garden and both lived to a great age.

(Author's Collection; Rosa Stevens)

UPWARE

This is the once-famous inn, The Lord Nelson, built under thatch in 1811 but put under corrugated iron in the 1890s. It was re-christened the Five Miles from Anywhere — No Hurry in the 1860s by a rumbustious Cambridge graduate, Richard Ramsey Fielder, who described himself as His Majesty the King of Upware. Fielder came to drink and sport with the bargees and lightermen but after leaving the district he lived a sober, responsible life and wrote good poetry. From 1851 the inn was the headquarters of the Upware Republic, a society of Cambridge undergraduates, including Samuel Butler, seeking respite from their studies. This view dates from early this century when my maternal grandparents, Ben and Kate Read, kept the inn. The commercial river traffic was in decline then but they prospered there with land to produce their own vegetables, ducks and chickens. They held fishing rights and made a fair profit out of the ferry which they hired from the brewers for £7 a year. Their charges for its use were as follows: a penny for a person on foot, twopence with a bicycle, fourpence with pony and trap, sixpence with horse and cart and twopence a head for cattle, it being not uncommon to carry a dozen at a time. Such a full load, however, sometimes sank the ferry, leaving the cattle to cross by themselves — or go back!

(Author's Collection)

27

BARWAY

This tiny hamlet within Soham parish but nearer to the Wicken boundary is on a rise on the opposite side of the Great Ouse from Little Thetford. It had its school and its ancient church that is now a private home, its seats having been transferred to Wicken church. Soham Lode passes Barway to its junction with the Ouse where stood this Harrimere Mill, a fine example of its kind, complete with accommodation for its overseer. It drained the land that was formerly Soham Mere but it was pulled down in 1917 in favour of more modern methods. A mill such as this, which was the standard method of drainage before the steam age, stands in Wicken Fen, restored from the original used to drain the turf-pits. This scene dates from early this century.

(Cambridgeshire Collection)

28

BARWAY AND LITTLE THETFORD

We are looking towards Ely about eighty years ago and private ferry boats await on the Ouse below Harrimere Mill with Little Thetford pumping station on the left. The picture was taken near the official chain ferry used for cattle, horses and carts and those who had no boats. Little Thetford by the A10 to Ely was once separated from it by water. A few more than two hundred lived there at the time of this photograph but development has increased that to 430 today. Thetford engine house was demolished in the early 1960s.

(Cambridgeshire Collection)

Main Street. (looking North) Stretham.

STRETHAM

Wicken touches fen level over the river Cam, from where it is two miles to Stretham and the A10. Many of its visitors are looking for Stretham Old Engine, the one steam pumping station preserved intact and open to the public by the Old West River. A trust was formed with Cyril Clarke the custodian and superintendent of drainage at the centre just in time to save the engine from being cut to pieces and the building felled. Built in 1831, it now contains a museum for its visitors. The pump was on standby duty during the Second World War but is no longer secure enough to function. With its cottages clustered about its rise Stretham is bigger than it looks to the passing traveller, who is usually on the A10 bypass. It is attractive at its centre where the picturesque church faces a square with a market cross. This is its main street looking north and churchwards in the 1920s with the White Lion public house on the left where the tenant was John Sindall, who also kept a butcher's shop just outside the picture on the left. When his wife died John was left with six daughters at home. He was succeeded at the inn by Ada Leach who liked to be first with the local news. The carrier on the left is Ted Lowe. The White Lion was restored as a home a few years ago for the Topsy and Tim authors, Jean and the late Gareth Adamson.

(Cambridgeshire Collection)

STRETHAM

Before the bridge was built over the Old West river on the Wicken road there was a ferry for the few who needed it. Stretham ferry, however, was the term used for the crossing at the A10 Cambridge road. A bridge replaced it but a new bridge replaced that in 1928 while the Wicken road bridge was being built. I well recall being present in April 1928 when Wicken bridge over the Cam was being tested as we see here at Stretham ferry, using the heaviest mobile weights at hand. This bridge has now been superseded by another where the A10 has been straightened. This 1928 bridge is now used by fishermen and those visiting or leaving the Lazy Otter inn, which at the time of the event depicted here was called The Royal Oak.
(Cambridgeshire Collection)

WILBURTON

A mile beyond Stretham on the hill it shares with Haddenham, this village has great charm and dignity and it is small wonder its residents bestirred themselves recently to oppose a new village on its fringes. The fens below Wilburton have yielded many relics of human habitation, some in gold and bronze. The Burystead in Station Road, built in 1607 on the site of an earlier manor, is an impressive building. Its replacement as the manor house in the 17th century, also in Station Road, was rebuilt between 1848 and 1851 but was left empty for seven years before becoming the home of the Pell family, who had succeeded to the manor in 1817. One member, Mr. Beauchamp Pell, lives in the rectory here today. The manor house is now a school and the station on the Ely — St. Ives line fell to Dr. Beeching. In this view we see, c.1910, the old village school at the end. It opened in 1855 but gave way to a new school long ago. Under the tree is the smithy of William Ellis Hudson and Sons and beyond that is Hazell's shop, but the next two cottages were destroyed by fire. The foreground cottages remain in a village where the church enchants the eye.

(Cambridgeshire Collection)

WILBURTON

Joseph Hazell kept a shop in Wilburton from the 1870s and it was continued by his daughter Martha until 1934; but this, early this century, is the shop owned by Joseph's nephew, Walter Hazell, from 1884 to 1936. It was previously owned by William Flanders. Walter sold groceries and drapery and measured for suits. He also made his own ginger beer. He was succeeded in the business by his son Harold Walter and Harold's wife Kathleen Mary while their son Alistair assisted for 17 years. VAT was the last straw for Harold and he closed the shop in 1979. Happily it was recently redesigned as a shop with post office for Mr. Roger Brew and his family. In this picture Walter Hazell stands on the right with his wife and children with an assistant in the doorway.

(Cambridgeshire Collection)

WILBURTON

Bovine miracles happened in Wilburton. In 1881 a calf was born here with three tongues to a cow owned by Christopher Sulman while on February 22nd, 1900 this cow belonging to farmer George Sharpe gave birth to these five healthy calves. Half the kingdom heard of this and the two vets in attendance rightly concur that a celebratory cigar apiece after the succession of deliveries is not out of place. Mr. Sharpe, with the beard, and his wife Sarah (nee Sulman, which is a long-established Wilburton name) and their son Harry, clearly agree. Only the exhausted cow feels she has done enough for one day.
(Cambridgeshire Collection)

Aldreth, Haddenham. J 5244. (W. E. Green's Series.)

ALDRETH

This small village below Haddenham rings of history, for here, when it was known as Lindon, William the Conqueror's invaders were thrice repelled by Hereward the Wake before the construction of a causeway enabled them to reach Ely. The Roman road from Cambridge northwards merely supplemented this route until it was brought up to a higher standard in the late 18th century. The road downhill into Aldreth arrives at a drove, leaving the village almost as peaceful today as we see it here in 1911, where the silence is broken only by the clop of heavy horses, the crunch of tumbrel wheels and probably the crowing of the occasional cockerel. In the street George Thulborn is transporting a load of the rich stuff to the fields of Willow Farm.

(Cambridgeshire Collection)

35

ALDRETH

Although little more than a hamlet, Aldreth had its own football team between the wars, competing against other small clubs from the small Isle villages. Here from the 1920s are, left to right, back row: E. Jackson, R. Gothard, E. Peacock, E. Benton. Middle: E. Pode, B. Burton, H. Careless, H. Hemment, A. Thulborn. Front: A. Thulborn, J. Pettingale. With a name like Careless you need courage to be a footballer!

(Cambridgeshire Collection)

HADDENHAM

We come here to the mountian of the fens, reaching 120 feet above sea level at its peak, offering a perspective of the fens that can be bettered only from the top of Ely cathedral. Soaked in the low-level haze the long island is a welcoming sight from the bank of the New Bedford river between Earith and Sutton. The climb in this photograph from about 80 years ago is in Station Road — minus its station now, of course — which was helpful enough to those in a hurry to catch a train. It is little changed today and Haddenham is richly endowed with fine old mellow buildings. The population now is approaching 3,000. The 13th century Holy Trinity church crowning this view has been rather crudely restored and its obvious need of a spire led to fund raising to that end. This, however, had an unfortunate outcome. The funds were embezzled by one who fled to America and was never heard of again.

(Cambridgeshire Collection)

HADDENHAM

Hospital Sundays were a feature of fen village life until the Second World War, bringing, in most cases, a huge proportion of the population together wearing their Sunday best to contribute money to the hospitals when there was no National Health Service to provide for them. After modest contribution schemes had been introduced these parades still continued as much out of social need and tradition as for the original purpose. They coincided with the village feasts and the band led a column to church and back consisting of civil armies, decorated floats and wagons and the huge banners of the various friendly societies. Here the column arrives at Haddenham green in the 1920s. The man with the bicycle in the foreground has kept faith with his carbide lamp, but many found these irksome to maintain and put up with the fainter glow of paraffin. At a later date I travelled to this parade on the crossbar of my father's bicycle.
(Cambridgeshire Collection)

QUEEN ADELAIDE

This hamlet near Ely on the road to Prickwillow, intersected by the rail routes to King's Lynn and Norwich and the river Ouse, was the site chosen for the Ely Beet Sugar Factory in 1925. Farmers soon overcame their suspicion of this crop when the returns became apparent and increased their acreage in spite of the labour involved in growing it. The plants had to be chopped out into bunches and these singled, mostly by women and boys as a casual job, crawling along or bending over the land for between threepence and sixpence a row according to length. At first the harvesting involved digging out each root with a two-tined fork, ridding each of its soil, lopping and transporting them by horse and cart to roadside, railside or riverside heaps. Later the beetplough helped matters. The permit system that still operates regulated deliveries to the factory, ensuring that harvesting carries on into the depth of winter. Transport firms undertook deliveries, but farmers soon came to acquire their own lorries, such as this on the weighbridge at Ely in the 1920s. The factory closed in 1975, forcing the Isle farmers to deliver to Bury St. Edmunds or Wissington.

(Cambridgeshire Collection)

39

PRICKWILLOW

This was once a tiny settlement beside the river Ouse, but when the course of this river was changed in 1829, Prickwillow was expanded over the silt banks of the old course. A school was built in 1862 and a church in 1866, both on piles. It is six miles to Isleham across the fen and two windmills once drained it along with Soham Mere, but once the river was redirected towards Littleport a steam pumping engine was installed at the head of the drain in 1831. A second station was built beside it in 1880 and its steam pump was replaced by diesel in 1924. Both buildings appear here on this hospital Sunday occasion in May 1923, the old one on the right. So, no, the people had not just emerged from the chapel on the left although the similarity between lay chapels of the period and pumping stations was often striking. The tributes in this one were to steam. 'Steam, mighty steam, ascends the throne / And Reigns, Lord Paramount, alone,' wrote the versifying Commissioner of Drainage, having it inscribed on a tablet on the Burnt Fen pumping station nearby, which has been demolished. Open weekends are held at Prickwillow, enabling visitors to see the preserved pumping engine working.

(Cambridgeshire Collection)

LITTLEPORT

Five miles east of Ely on its own rise, the urban village of Littleport keeps its fame for the hunger riots of 1816, when heavy taxation drove a band of men to march on the Bishop of Ely demanding support. After some rioting and looting they were halted by the militia from Bury St. Edmunds and five of their number were selected as ringleaders, sentenced and hanged while others were deported. There is a memorial to these martyrs to a cause on the church of St. Mary in Ely. This small harbour above the swamp expanded into a small town. Few of its secular buildings are old. Just above 4,000 people lived here at the time of this photograph, c.1905. It shows Main Street with the town hall, built in 1879, at the end of the corner of Granby Street. Farther along into Victoria Street is the village hall built in 1880, to which a day centre was added in 1982. On the extreme right is the harness and saddle shop of Charles Defew while the stately house next to it was the home of William Dallis, potato merchant. The cyclists are standing near the Alfa Cycle and Motor Works owned by Alfred Adams. That is a station delivery cart in the distance and Littleport station, proposed in 1845, remains on the London — Lynn line.

(Cambridgeshire Collection)

41

LITTLEPORT

Sandhill Bridge over the Ouse at Littleport was originally a wooden structure named, most likely, after Sir Miles Sandys who was Lord of the Manor here in the 17th century. It was his plan to straighten the Ouse from Ely to Littleport two hundred years before it was actually done. The wooden bridge was replaced by this iron one in 1890 where, in August 1903, the first Littleport water sports drew a large crowd to watch eager participants. Thereafter, on the third day of the village feast, they were held annually. It was all for fun for locally born amphibians who competed in underwater swims and dived for thrown plates and were entitled to feel free at the end to tip the officials out of their boats. The barges gave access to deep water leaving the crowd to watch in safety. This was the event in 1906.
(Cambridgeshire Collection)

LITTLEPORT

Joe Atkins is well remembered in Littleport today and is recalled by some who never knew him. Living in an idyllic thatched cottage, long since demolished, in Wellington Street, Joe was a joiner, carpenter, undertaker and wheelwright who was also very active in church matters. He was verger to St. George's church and its acting clerk and Sunday school teacher with a great interest in the history and welfare of his parish. Joe stands here beside the first cart he ever made, exhibiting but modest pride, in 1902. It was fitted with iron tyres for general use. For genteel purposes rubber tyres were fitted, the sound of the wheels telling the tale.

(Cambridgeshire Collection)

LITTLE DOWNHAM

Downham-in-the-Isle is the alternative name, on the northern side of Ely's rise three miles from the city centre. From here the descent, on the way to the small community at Pymoor, is some fifty feet within half a mile. Here was built the palace used by the Bishops of Ely during summer. It was rebuilt for Bishop John Alcock between 1486-1501 and the remains at what is now the Tower Farm Riding Centre are all from this period. The palace was celebrated for its grand interior. Downham is unusual for having more shops today than when this picture was taken about 1918. In that year the population was 1,887 and in 1990 it was 2,160. William Woods Green was a harness maker here from the 1870s. This is his shop in Main Street where he was succeeded by his brother Charles who was in turn succeeded by his son Alfred William (Fred). Keeping up with the age they extended to cycles and motors and lasted into the 1960s. Fred Green stands on the left and Charles second from the left with two assistants. The shop is now a private home.

(Cambridgeshire Collection)

LITTLE DOWNHAM

At a time when hospital Sundays were flourishing elsewhere, Downham's was in decline and many local people wanted to drop it. Littleport band leads this token parade along Main Street in the 1930s, with tents erected for the village feast celebrations. There would be a fair too down Eagles Lane, the turning this side of the Fox and Hounds public house jutting out on the left, where Leonard Plumb was mine host. The inn was closed soon afterwards to become a private house. This caught fire on November 8th 1974 and Mrs. Ruth Young died from the smoke fumes. The house was then thoroughly renovated. Beyond the tents in this picture is the Baptist Sunday school built in 1930, on the corner of Chapel Lane, down which the Baptist chapel is now closed and boarded up. There have been few alterations to this view but the house on the immediate left has gone. The boys on the right have their minds on the ice cream brought in by tricycle cart.

(Cambridgeshire Collection)

45

COVENEY

Here is a miniature Ely, safe on its own little island four miles away, its church of St. Peter ad Vicula built some five hundred years before Vermuyden's drainage scheme. Boats were used to approach it then. The fen road below Ely twists and turns to lengthen the journey, but Coveney sits charmingly on its hill. It was once a very long parish but Vermuyden cut it in two. Its other half on the other side of the Bedford rivers, no less than five miles away but nearer sixteen round by road, has grown much bigger. In 1819 there were uprisings here, as elsewhere in the fens, when the poor of the parish strove to take possession of the charity lands to share among themselves. Magistrates had nine of their number arrested and the cause was frustrated. Facing Ely with no obstructions to spoil the view from Main Street, this village shop and post office, seen in 1921, was owned by Herbert William Baker, whose wife Clara and daughter Alma, who still lives in the village, are standing at the door. This is now a house, not much altered, but the cottage next door has lost the shape of its dormer windows. Today, like so many small villages, Coveney has no shop, no post office and no school.

(Cambridgeshire Collection)

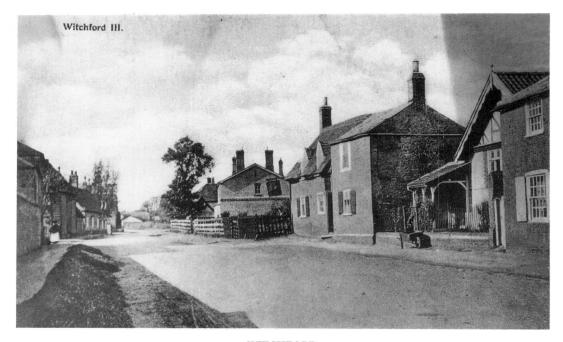

Witchford III.

WITCHFORD

Three miles west of Ely on the old Chatteris route and bypassed by the A142, which leaves it almost as quiet as in this view from early this century, Witchford is on high ground within Ely's rise, reaching some eighty feet above fen level. It has few ancient buildings apart from St. Andrew's church beside the one long, undulating street with modern cul-de-sacs leading off. But it was here that Ely's monks first met William the Conqueror, who inflicted such heavy taxes on the small population that the church's treasure had to be melted down to pay them. Its importance grew to become the centre of the Witchford Hundred, a geographical division originally based on the presence of a hundred families. 150 years ago the village was known for its poor hygiene due to an open drain alongside the street. The 400 inhabitants at the time this picture was taken have stretched to above 1,500 now. This westwards view, taken near the church, is not much altered today. The cottage and St. Andrew's hall on the right remain. The next two cottages have gone from which the Shoulder of Mutton public house shifted to the house beyond. Eighty years ago the landlord was John Downs. The far cottages also remain, but not those buildings on the left.

(Cambridgeshire Collection)

WENTWORTH

This charming hamlet is right in the centre of Ely's isle and was at the time of the Domesday Book a substantial village and it was large enough in the 13th century to justify the building of its attractive church dedicated to St. Peter. It was extensively restored in 1868 and is at present being modified to serve also as a village hall. Amazingly by the year 1428 there were only nine people living in Wentworth. Enclosure, which affected it more drastically than other parishes hereabouts, may have been the cause. It had its school from 1873 to accommodate more than fifty children but the number was down to sixteen in 1922 and the school was closed, the children travelling the short distance to Witchford. The building shown here survived the Second World War as a private dwelling, but its days as a public house were secure enough in 1917 when this photograph was taken. The landlord then was George Dewey. Having lost his wife he took in a housekeeper, Edith Hughes, and later married her and she succeeded him along with her brother Isaac and they saw out its days as a public house. Mr. and Mrs. Fish followed as tenants and they by three sisters and a brother of the Bishop family, a member of which now occupies a new house on the site. There was once a small pond in front of the Fish and Duck which was opposite the church off Main Street.

(Cambridgeshire Collection)

WITCHAM

Witcham stands on its own modest hill below the Witchford — Sutton road, its cottages clustered about the 13th century church of St. Martin. Its tower is massively buttressed and broad in relation to height. Schools were provided here from the year 1562, with a John Fernley licensed as schoolmaster, but no truly adequate school was provided until 1873 and today there is no school. This view of the high street in 1929 shows the Bricklayers' Arms on the right, tenanted by the Leach brothers. It was felled a few years ago and a new house put on the site. The small flat building beyond was also a cottage and the thatched one beyond that remains in modified form, minus the thatch. 'Windrush', the cottage opposite, is the home of Alf Sharpe of sharp recall and in front of it we see the grocery cart of Tom Weedon, come all the way from Chatteris. Other tradesmen came in this way, one from March. At this time the two modes of transport were of about equal importance in this area, but before long all such travelling vendors were motorised.

(Cambridgeshire Collection)

49

SUTTON-IN-THE-ISLE

At the western tip of Ely's isle, Sutton shines above the flat fens like a sunny promontory to the homecoming seafarer, its unique church the spiritual lighthouse signalling welcome. Its architect was clearly inspired by the space around. The tower of this decorated gem, built for Bishop Barnett of Ely between 1366 and 1373, has two octagons and is known locally as the pepperbox. Sutton rises eighty feet above the fens and its High Street is long and undulating. The view has changed little since this turn of the century photograph. All the buildings on the right remain. The dutch-gabled house, minus its ivy, is now the doctor's home and surgery. The second bay window on the left has become a shop and there have been changes farther along. Sutton's population in 1911 was 1,531 but it is more than double that now.
(Cambridgeshire Collection)

SUTTON-IN-THE-ISLE

There is a California on the Norfolk coast, another near Ipswich and a small patch near Little Downham is called the same and as Sutton dips towards fen level and Earith it becomes America. The hard route outwards originally turned right a little farther along from here, going through Sutton Gault and crossing the Bedford rivers and washes, but later this drove became the main route, catching up with the New Bedford bank and following it to Hermitage Lock. The scene is a lot changed today but instantly recognisable.

(Cambridgeshire Collection)

SUTTON-IN-THE-ISLE

We jump forward to 1947 and the dire floods that afflicted the fens after that severe and prolonged post-war winter. 'Operation Noah's Ark' was mounted by the military, when there were plenty of spare men available, to stem the floods and ease the plight of the homeless. The Ouse burst its banks in mid-March but the floods had eased by the end of the month and reoccupation and rebuilding began. There are many photographs of half-submerged houses and people and animals marooned, such as were previously recorded in 1937. This is America again, near the same spot, the small building on the right being in both views. The last great threat to marshland occurred in 1953 when the sea-walls collapsed as in earlier times. With sea levels apparently rising let it never be said it could not happen again!
(Cambridgeshire Collection)

SUTTON-IN-THE-ISLE

Like most fen and marshland villages and towns Sutton celebrated its feast Sunday with a hospital parade. It was unusually late here, in the third week in September. Figures were published to show the need for such fund-raising and the activities were largely self-supportive. For instance, in 1927 there were 57 Sutton people receiving hospital treatment and there was only a modest contribution scheme to support it. The parade of 1928 raised £30-13s-2d, a goodly sum then. This parade took place on September 30th, by which time many locals had subscribed to other village parades. Sutton also persisted with a Peace Day parade and sports well after the First World War. This one, led by the Ely G.E.R. Band, took place on July 17th, 1920, with septuagenarian H. Ibberson mounted on a grey horse marshalling the procession of fancy dress competitors from the National Schools at 1p.m. to the sports ground at Mepal Road. 1,400 paid for admission to the sports events when the population was 1,476! Dancing to the railway band followed until 10.30p.m. and the money generated simply funded the event the next year. Such was the community spirit in our fen villages then.

(Cambridgeshire Collection)

MEPAL

Sutton is bypassed by the A142 to Chatteris, as is its much smaller neighbour, Mepal to its huge advantage. For a long time the number of people living here closer to fen level stayed close to the number of days in the year, but there are now nearly 500 residents. Fires in 1856, 1858, 1863 and 1865 took away many of its old buildings and reduced the population when it was nearing 500 before. Mepal is eight miles from Ely and four and a half from Chatteris and the old road now ends at the New Bedford river where the Three Pickerels inn still thrives. The old wooden bridge over the New Bedford in this view from c.1895 was replaced by a concrete one in 1930. The buildings on the right have gone. Beyond them to the right was also the Black Bull public house, now gone, but beyond that the old ferryman's cottage is still there. At this point Mepal remains as peaceful as we see it here.

(Central Divisional Library, King's Lynn; the Taylor Slide Collection)

THE VILLAGE PUMP, MEPAL

MEPAL

This scene in Mepal High Street just after the First World War is now much altered. Not only fires reduced the old cottages. The one on the left remains but much nearer our time the next three were removed. The small one tucked away behind the pump, which has also gone without trace, was the White Hart public house. The cottage behind the cart is still there but the others have gone. Sally Tholborn stands left with her children, while the little girl enjoys her leisurely ride in the cart.

(Cambridgeshire Collection)

55

MANEA

This was the other half of Coveney, grown much bigger than its parent. Isolated too on its lower island, Manea has on its south side a small rise known as Charlemont where King Charles I had planned a small town, an aim thwarted by his untimely end. The church of St. Nicholas was built in 1875 to replace one built in 1791, which had replaced an earlier one where foundations were insecure. We live in a time of redundant churches so it is surprising to discover Manea provided itself with a new Primitive Methodist chapel in 1990, this replacing the one shown here c.1910 in Station Road, which had been closed for thirty years. Meanwhile the worshippers continued in the St. Nicholas church schoolroom. The cottages on the extreme left and right still stand, as does the one beyond the chapel that was Fred Stokes' butcher's shop. Beyond the next cottage shown here was an old washhouse, beyond which stood a shop used by rock-maker William Thompson, who attended fairs. The people gaze but there is nothing posed about this scene. Manea's station on the London — Lynn line is still used.

(Cambridgeshire Collection)

DODDINGTON

Off the A141 past Chatteris, Doddington was once the largest Cambridgeshire parish, taking in March, Wimblington and Benwick and covering some 31,800 acres. It sits on fenland's largest island after Ely, four miles long and a mile and a half wide, but a mere twenty five feet above sea level at its highest. The living was once the largest in the land, where one of the incumbents was Christopher Tye, organist to Queen Elizabeth I. This is New Street c.1914 showing the clocktower erected to commemorate Queen Victoria's Diamond Jubilee in 1897. The cost to the county was £80 but the spire and weathervane were added after 1911. In March 1937 the county surveyor suggested the clocktower should be moved to open up the highway and in 1938 this was done with great care by builder Bert Collins, who had already done a fine job of rebuilding the village's tiny Round House. Lead roofing replaced the tiles on the clocktower and the railings were added later. The new site is roughly where the photographer is standing here. The formal handing over took place in November 1938. The George public house behind, now rebuilt, was, along with The Three Tuns, among the first to provide customers with wireless entertainment.

(Cambridgeshire Collection)

HOSPITAL SUNDAY AT DODDINGTON 1912 A558

DODDINGTON

Long divorced from its other villages, Doddington in 1911 had 1,486 inhabitants and this has increased but little today. When most hospital Sundays were over and harvest festivals were nigh, Doddington, along with Sutton, celebrated theirs. It was an occasion not so much for best clothes, but new clothes worn for the first time. Exiles came home to be welcomed with special teas and the band or bands was as near as village people wanted to get to pomp and drama. It was the climax of the social year, such as it was, and the weather held for them in this scene from 1912, filling the road reserved for traffic today.

(Cambridgeshire Collection)

BENWICK

Reached by the B1093 via Doddington or by the road alongside the Fortyfoot river, or Vermuyden's Drain, Benwick is a rather drab little village built on shingle yet on fen level, giving too little support to some of its buildings. None of these is very old, including the church, while the lay chapel only reveals itself as such when you draw close. By the drain route you come first to Swingbrow, where this photograph typifying the fen landscape was taken in the 1890s. No exiled Dutchman, traditionally working here in the cause of drainage, would have felt homesick in this setting, surely. Beezling drainage mill is on the left and Westmoor mill on the right and not only the farmers of today sought to remove trees and hedges. The turn off to Benwick is two miles along.

(Cambridgeshire Collection)

WIMBLINGTON

This former part of Doddington parish a mile away has long been a proud village in its own right. Yet it is not old. The Hill is hardly that but there stands St. Peter's church built in 1874, with but one bell in its tower. On the left in this view from c.1916 is the Old Unicorn public house owned by Ogden and Sons of the Sun Brewery in March. Their first tenant here was John Henry Parkinson, who was also the village coalman. He was there from 1905 to 1933. Greene King took over the inn and installed two tenants before the premises were converted into a private house. It was demolished in 1968 and in its place stands an above average development called Governess Close. The fine houses in the centre and on the right remain. Beyond the centre house is the entrance to the Thomas Eaton school, now for juniors and infants only. Eaton bequeathed two houses and 8½ acres of land for a school in 1715 but it was not built for exactly one hundred years. Even then it was not well built and a new one, the present, replaced it in 1924. Wimblington was adjudged the best kept village in north Cambridgeshire in both 1975 and 1976.

(Cambridgeshire Collection)

THREE HOLES

When riverside and wayside inns were frequent and popular this one, shown in the 1920s, was both. On the A1101 on the south edge of Upwell, which is wedged between Cambridgeshire and Norfolk, this hamlet is so called from the shape of the bridge over the Sixteenfoot Drain. The photographer clearly recognised that his car would become a charming period piece and left it there handy for his refreshment afterwards. Mine host here at this time was Robert Chapman but his dear old home has now gone, leaving a mobile caravan on an otherwise empty site. The Red Hart, beyond the far cottages, provides the refreshment here now.

(Wisbech and Fenland Museum; Henry Coates)

UPWELL

Upwell and Outwell, linked by the Well Creek down the middle with one side in Cambridgeshire and the other in Norfolk, could be nowhere but the very heart of the fen country. In 1917, the travelling writer, John James Hissey, set down his unfavourable impressions of Upwell. Arriving from Wisbech by car after his journey had been disrupted by the Wisbech — Upwell tram service he described it as a succession of commonplace houses like a town street that had lost itself in the country. He might have least have recognised that Upwell was well on the way to becoming a town until Wisbech developed ahead of it. It remains one of the longest villages in England, welcoming in its character and atmosphere. In this view from 1902, looking over the creek, which after years of neglect is now well maintained by the Well Creek Trust, the building on the right was used for the doctor's surgery. The cottages next to it were owned by Joel Parker, a builder, and the tallest bulding beyond these was the Globe Inn.
(Cambridgeshire Collection)

OUTWELL

Outwell's population in 1911 was 376 compared to 2,064 in Upwell. This photograph dates from about this time with the tram depot on the left and Cooper's stores on the right, with the proprietor in the doorway. Mr. Cooper's wife Lydia, then his son Bert with his wife Grace, succeeded him at this shop. Behind the little tram booking office which is still there, is Cox's bakery with the bakehouse behind, a scene graced by St. Clement's church. The shop is still used on this corner. It was at this tram depot in July 1932 that a man backed a wagon on to the tramline where it was struck by a tram and somehow severed his leg. He died shortly afterwards.
(Cambridgeshire Collection)

OUTWELL

The Wisbech — Upwell tramway was opened on Monday, August 20th, 1883, but the line was not completed through to Upwell until Monday, September 8th, 1884. It was used for passengers and freight, in particular farm and horticultural produce and coal. For a long time the fare all the way was twopence. This unique service in the fens is well documented. Drivers and conductors were used to having their photographs taken. The steam trams were replaced by diesel locomotives in 1952 but road transport soon replaced the service and it closed in 1966. Here, c.1910, the tram has just arrived at Outwell Depot and Cooper's stores from Upwell. It might have been a tourist attraction today, like the Nene Valley Railway near Peterborough.

(Cambridgeshire Collection)
(Wisbech and Fenland Museum; Henry Coates)

3668 Emneth Village.

EMNETH

Nearing Wisbech via the A1101 we come to Emneth off the main road where the church tower is supported by an encircling chain embedded in its walls. In the centre of this small village the shop now owned by Mr. P.H. Hodges was Herbert Edgoose's store, shown here in the 1920s. He was the typical village shopkeeper never wanting to be stumped for any item and here he displays many services — telephone kiosk, post office, petrol, foods, tobacco, confectionery and hardware, motor oil, slot machines and the bakery behind. Mr. Edgoose, who moved on to Sutton Bridge, was warmly recalled for me by Frank Quince living nearby, who also outlined the history of the mill behind. Built in 1832 for the miller W.A. Forth, it passed to W. Shepherd, W. Racey and James Frederick Racey, who was the last miller there. These men also owned and supplied the bakery. The four sails were destroyed by fire in 1912. James Racey rebuilt the damaged mill, taking the tower up six feet and installing a gas engine to power the mill. Sometimes he let the boy Frank Quince crank the engine for him, on the understanding that the flame had to be blue before the engine could start. The mill once sheltered a criminal on the run for a few anxious hours. It was eventually demolished and the site purchased by Mr. Peter Russell and then R.W. Thomas, motor engineers, who occupy the site and the garage opposite today.

(Wisbech and Fenland Museum; Henry Coates)

Elm Village & Church, Wisbech.

ELM

This village adjoining Wisbech is as old as its church in many parts. The church is a fine example of 13th century architecture, although its tower battlements were added later. The builders of the Victorian church here held lesser views of longevity, for their building has lost its shape to the soil. Gone are so many of the orchards that once surrounded this dignified village, whose name may well derive from 'eel' rather than the tree, but there are trees aplenty here and fine gardens. Newer developments look over-arranged and urban in their tastes. Needham Hall here is built over the site of an historic mansion and it was here that Cromwell is reputed to have slept on a hard table rather than the bed offered him so that he should fare no better than his accompanying troops.

(Cambridgeshire Collection)

FRIDAY BRIDGE

There is hardly an undeveloped gap between Elm and Friday Bridge, which were one and the same parish until the ecclesiastical separation on July 3rd, 1860. Friday Bridge, however, can in no way match Elm for the rich character of its buildings and the tree-lined road in from March gives no indication of the bareness within. Its church of St. Mark was built also in 1860 but it was poorly founded and its tower and spire are gradually pointing away from Heaven to earth, along with the rest of the building. It vies with the steeple of St. Laurence in Surfleet, Lincolnshire as the Pisa of the fens. Friday Bridge has two other dominant towers. Enhancing the centre of this plain village is this clocktower, built of brick and faced with stucco, erected in 1924 to commemorate the 24 local dead of the First World War — a dreadful toll from such a small community, but not far above average.

(Cambridgeshire Collection)

67

FRIDAY BRIDGE

The third and most dominant tower in the centre of this village, dwarfing the adjacent clocktower and memorial, belongs to the Wisbech Water Works and was built in 1894. Serving a wide area, it was powered by the engine shown here, supervised by George Maile, in the 1930s. George, who died in 1949 when his son was only twelve, was succeeded by Henry Warby in this job. This engine has long since been removed. Happily the voices of children at play in the school playground in Maltmas Lane still uplift the atmosphere in Friday Bridge, whose name derives from the monks' day for eating fish.

(District Library, Wisbech; Lilian Ream)

WALSOKEN

We are approaching Marshland, reclaimed from the sea long ago leaving land rich for cultivation, providing wealth enough to create some of the finest churches in England. On April 2nd, 1934 the larger part of Walsoken was amalgamated with Wisbech and a great public occasion was made of it. No public holiday was declared, but schoolchildren were freed to attend the ceremonies from 11 a.m. through to the roasting of an ox in the park in the evening, followed by display of fireworks. New boundary stones had been prepared, put in place and draped with union jacks for solemn unveilings and here we see the ex-warden of Walsoken Urban District Council performing the ritual of handing over to the mayor of Wisbech, Joseph Smith. This stone is just inside the railings of the entrance to the park in Park Street. The dignitaries lunched together in the Rose and Crown hotel and the damp weather did nothing to spoil the day. No matter that the spit inside the ox broke during the roasting, the meat was cooked, the mayor auctioned the first slices for good causes, raising £21−12s and sent some of the meat to the Poor Law Institution. The amalgamation had been long considered and had its advantages, the communities being so adjacent.

(District Library, Wisbech; Lilian Ream)

69

WALSOKEN

This was the heart of orchard country, but the times are bad for our fruitgrowers. There were rosebeds here too of transporting fragrance and in spring and summer the landscape was alight with blossom and blooms. Walsoken church is one of the most admired in East Anglia, with splendidly carved Norman arcades and painted angels looking down from the roof and with ornate 15th century screens between the aisles and chapels. The seven sacraments are depicted on the 14th century font where was baptised Thomas Herring (1693—1757) a native of Wisbech educated at Jesus and Corpus Christi Colleges, Cambridge, who won an early renown as a preacher and after several ecclesiastical appointments became Archbishop of Canterbury in 1748. The melodic bells were cast in nearby Downham Market. This view dates from the 1920s.

(Wisbech and Fenland Museum; Henry Coates)

STRAWBERRY PICKERS

This is how it was and still is on a much reduced scale in fen and marshland. Market forces have hit the growers where the soil is right and the spirit willing and you just have to wonder why. 'Pick your own' is the theme today from the remaining strawberry growers but at the time of this photograph in 1908 such a recourse was unthinkable. High flavour is essential but cropping and size equally so. In 1931 a grower from Walsoken, Mr. L.G. Sleight, produced 24 strawberries that turned the scales at more than two pounds and that made him more enemies than friends among the other growers. You can still follow your nose to the fenland strawberry fields in June and July and still buy from the roadside stalls, but the growers tell you sad tales.

(Central Divisional Library, King's Lynn; Bowskill Collection)

THE FRUITPICKERS

They came to Wisbech in trainloads from London to pick fruit from the vast orchards surrounding the town between the wars. Today there is not even a station for them to arrive at in Wisbech and many fewer orchards to justify the journey by car. They arrived like hop-pickers into Kent to enjoy a working, health-enhancing communal exercise in the sun and they brought their children who had to be supervised. In came undergraduates from Cambridge, many using their own means of transport as seen here in this inspired photograph taken in 1928, their chosen job being to supervise the creches for small children to leave the parents unhindered in their work. A self-contained hamlet was built in Elm to accommodate many of the pickers.

(District Library, Wisbech; Lilian Ream)

GUYHIRN

One-street villages are common enough in the flat country, but one-sided streets are rare. Guyhirn is built alongside the high bank of the river Nene which continues to Wisbech six miles away and The Wash. So many photographs of this village taken by Margaret George (1899–1983), who lived here between 1918 and 1949 where her father was the local vicar, were set against this grassy bank where sheep graze, if not entirely safely from the tidal waters. Here she captures to perfection the atmosphere of the village railway station in 1928 where the mother beguiles the restless child and the man hopes for sound and sight of the train. Dr. Beeching closed what had begun as the Great Eastern and Northern Joint Railway to Wisbech.

(Margaret George; courtesy of Brian Payne)

MURROW

A small village, this, barely three miles along the B1187 from Guyhirn, where this event took place on June 4th, 1932, in the Manor House field owned by G.F. Coupland. Village sports meetings were very popular between the wars and this was the fourteenth annual meeting at Murrow involving athletic events, cycle racing, which was keenly competitive at the time, and an obstacle race for horses and riders. While galloping the horse round the course the rider had to remove the saddle and ride bareback carrying a bag of chaff! He had to put a tyre round the poor horse's neck and ride round again, remove the tyre, replace the saddle and race to the finishing post. Billy Sennitt of Upware won the big cycle race and the challenge cup outright. As a child he had undergone drastic operations on his legs and on doctor's orders used a cycle to strengthen them. He was forced to propel, gracelessly, with his insteps, but he learned to excel. If he was therefore something of a trick cyclist he was no match in this field for Chasewater Charlie from Truro, seen here entertaining the crowd with one of his strange assortment of cycles. Three years on the organisers had advanced to motorcycle tricksters and a tight wire act.

(District Library, Wisbech; Lilian Ream)

School & Jubilee Clock. PARSON DROVE.

PARSON DROVE

Near Murrow, Parson Drove is a long, scattered village built on a green drove that was wider than the present road. Here stood one of the last woad mills in England until 1910. Samuel Pepys came here on 17th and 18th September, 1663 and, of course, set down his impressions. They were unfavourable. He came to see to the affairs of his late aunt Beatrice and mentions his uncle Perkins, husband of another aunt, Jane Pepys, who were living in poverty at Parson Drove. Samuel lodged at the Swan Inn which much later, in 1834, belonged to Charles Boucher, a brewer, who altered it drastically. Pepys made it clear he loathed the fen country with its crude dwellings, rough roads and mosquitoes driving him to distraction and Parson Drove had more than its share of these. The village's separate existence from Leverington was recognised in 1784 when the Parson Drove School Board was established. The school seen here in the 1920s was replaced in 1933, the new one being dedicated to Alderman Payne of Cambridge. Seen here too across the North Level Drain is the jailhouse on the left, to which was added the clocktower to commemorate the Diamond Jubilee of Queen Victoria in 1897.

(District Library, Wisbech; Lilian Ream)

THORNEY TOLL

Between Guyhirn and Thorney on the A47 route to Peterborough is Thorney Toll, a small community of well-spaced cottages where once, of course, was the toll gate. Tollmen were as loved in their day as traffic wardens are now. Likened to spiders waiting to entwine flies, eliciting no sympathy from travellers going about their work or pleasure, still less from churchgoers and those attending funerals who were shown no mercy in their sorrow, they were encouraged to remain firm in their demands. Long after their heyday Margaret George travelled the short distance to Thorney Toll schoolroom to capture, poignantly, this moment of celebration among the young. The year is 1928 and the formally dressed taller young man is there to give instruction to youngsters wanting to keep up with their age.

(Margaret George; courtesy of Brian Payne)

THORNEY

We arrive at the Isle of Thorns, as early Christian ascetics called it. This is Thorney Abbey church, which is what remains of the great abbey that stood here over 500 years ago. The first monastic establishment here originated in the seventh century but it was sacked by the Danes and rebuilt in 972. It became a Benedictine abbey that suffered too as one of Hereward's strongholds. The Normans rebuilt here and over the succeeding centuries it grew prodigiously. At the Reformation the abbey had six aisles, a central tower and was 300 feet long. This church has a splendid window, a copy of one in Canterbury cathedral. Thorney's island rises some twenty feet above the surrounding fens, but the rise is not conspicuous while travelling the thirteen miles from Wisbech. This view dates from about 1910.

(Cambridgeshire Collection)

823 Wisbech Road, Thorney

THORNEY

For a long time Thorney was the sole property of successive Dukes of Bedford, that name so prominent in fen history. As a result the village still carries the look of a neatly planned and maintained estate. By late last century the Bedfords had provided over 300 of the village's 450 houses, built in a like style of brick and slate, released benignly on direct weekly tenancies rather than being made tied cottages. The school and other amenities were provided by the Bedfords too. They also raised the standards of hygiene here. Behind the cottages were washhouses and toilets in which was installed the original earth closets. Soil purchased from farmers was placed in a cupboard above the toilet and released by a 'flushing' device after use. A service was laid on for bucket collection and the contents were dumped in a heap on the fen and ultimately sold back to the farmers. Here we see, in the late 1920s, a row of Bedford houses beside the Wisbech road. The Wood sisters stand in front of their cottage which is behind the tree, while their aunt stands before her cottage for the distant camera. Behind her is the general store owned by Steve Parker. The cottages are privately owned now.

(Wisbech and Fenland Museum; Henry Coates)

THORNEY VILLAGE.

J. W. Badger, Peterborough and Hunstanton.

THORNEY

This is Abbey Place, Thorney, about 1910, and it has changed little. The buildings containing shops and businesses were built in the 1830s in a village where many other buildings are not as old as they first appear. At this time the trade occupants were as follows, from the left: the figures are standing before the window of William G. Bland the baker: the shopfront next was used by the Smith brothers, plumbers, to display their wares: a passage to the rear follows while the next shop was used by the Goodwin sisters selling sweets: Mr. Popeley the shoemaker comes next followed by a private house and, on the corner, William Cave, grocer, draper and later sub-postmaster. At this time, however, the post office was across the road in what were originally almshouses. Mr. Cave's old shop is now a house, as is the middle shopfront. Mr. Popeley's premises are now the post office run by Mr. R. Mackett and the plumbers' shop is now the property of Mr. D.L. Stokes, newsagent.

(Cambridgeshire Collection)

COATES

This small village near Whittlesey owes a lot to its central green. Around it today you will find too few old houses of character. Formed out of Whittlesey St. Mary in 1850, Coates already had its church of Holy Trinity in 1840. On the broad green in peculiar isolation stands the Wesley chapel, built in 1866, and nearer the road that divided the green stands this war memorial, unveiled on April 29th, 1920. Such was happening in most villages at this time after the plans had been laid and the money raised and the sincerity of the Armistice Day gatherings subsequently had to be seen to be believed. There had never been so many genuine mourners gathered together, never such longing for peace. After four years of deprivation and dreadful losses the nightmare was over and people were left craving only for the right to live simply with but modest celebration for reward.

(Cambridgeshire Collection)

WISBECH ST MARY

This parish three miles from Wisbech spreads wide, taking in pockets of existence far from its centre and church. On the B1441 from Guyhirn, it is at the heart of rich orchard country, or what is left of it. Corn growing instead is not altogether encouraged but at the time of this neatly arranged photograph the region could never grow enough. I use it to illustrate the beginning of machine harvesting, with the use of the reaper which left neat bunches of corn untied, the way it was also threshed. The grasscutter that preceded it simply left rows that had to be bunched and that was preceeded by scythe and sickle. The careful arrangement here illustrates 'fourses' time, that moment in the heat of afternoon when hot tea and slices of bread and butter were brought to the land, preceding the last stint of the day. Even after the binder had been introduced the reaper was used for cutting fodder crops like sangfoine and clover and for the second cutting of these for seed where binding was not necessary. This study is from the 1890s.

(Cambridgeshire Collection)

41 The Church, Leverington

LEVERINGTON

A mile north of Wisbech, Leverington is a large parish with the river Nene at its southern end. The smallholdings that sprouted here on rich farmland between 1901 and 1931 increased its population by 75% to almost 2,000 but it is now nearly 4,000. It has many fine houses and this splendid marshland church, one of so many, St. Leonards, founded on silt left by the sea, with a spire serving as a landmark for miles around. This is 13th century architecture at its finest. The 16th century Leverington Hall stands impressively nearby but there is also the later Leverington House on the seaward side of the old sea bank here and Park House where the first recorded owner was John Lumpkin (1655–1743). In its garden was a mulberry tree under which Goldsmith, it is claimed, may have written 'She Stoops to Conquer', using the name Lumpkin for his chief rustic character. Mrs. Hardcastle may have been dragged from the very pond nearby! A similar claim, however, is made for Leverington Rectory to make sure no outside claim gets a chance.

(District Library, Wisbech; Lilian Ream)

FOUR GOTES

Four miles nearer the sea on the A1101, Four Gotes is the hamlet I am able to choose to show the first of a sequence of corn-harvesting scenes in the 1930s. Four well-nurtured mares between them make the pulling of the binder look easy, but their exhaustion later in the long day told another story. In torrid weather they were pestered by swarms of flies and midges and their tails, left free to brush them off, could be a menace to human eyes. After being allowed to cool down in the yards or stables they were put out to graze and would instinctively contrive to be the far end of the pasture when the horsekeeper came to fetch them with halters in the morning. More often only three horses did the pulling, sometimes abreast, sometimes with one on traces in front as here, and more usually ridden by a boy just left school, small and light. I speak from experience in saying that it was like riding on a rocking boiler which left you, after the first day or two, wanting to sleep standing up!

(District Library, Wisbech; Lilian Ream)

NEWTON-IN-THE-ISLE

I talked to a fruitgrower here who had known far better days, when his trees were not pruned to look like great claws clutching at the ground from which pickers can gather the fruit without using ladders. Imports have hit the trade and land so suitable for fruit-growing is going to waste. Newton village has its charm, with fine trees and green spaces, but its little Colville school, built in 1930, stands cold and empty. The horse-leading boy in this scene from 1931 would be off school for the summer, helping out unpaid because like all village boys then he had to be involved. He was not necessary, for the pitcher could as well lead for himself between the corn-shocks. The boy would be required to cry, loud and clear: 'Hold ye!' in time honoured style before allowing the horse to move. Erring from this, his skin would be in danger! Once left school he would be entrusted to lead the horses between field and stackyard. Paid or unpaid he would be proud to hold these 'holdgeeing' jobs.

(District Library, Wisbech; Lilian Ream)

NEWTON-IN-THE-ISLE

The light work of the horse-leading was also suitable for girls imbued with farming from birth, with a fearless understanding of horses. Big farmhouses employed live-ins, girls and women of all work, who were generally quite happy to take a turn on the corn stack to release one of the men to begin work in the stockyard. Women who worked on the land did so by choice, prefering the open air, and I know some today who even now miss the jobs that were open to them then, such as that seen here and singling sugar beet, loathsome though this job might be to others. This girl knew how to avoid the ruts, ditches and gateposts and would hardly panic if on the way home they were met by a car or lorry that frightened the horse. This load is going to West's Farm at Newton and is a small load for a short journey. For longer distances the load would be higher and roped on, depending on the surfaces to be negotiated.

(District Library, Wisbech; Lilian Ream)

NEWTON-IN-THE-ISLE

Not all the corn was put into stacks. Threshing began during harvest, straight off the shock as here. This saved labour, but there was no better way to store corn than in the stack at this time. Not much of it was left loose in the granaries and not much in sacks because rats and mice would nibble into them and set men darning like grannies on wet days, using binder string and huge needles. The vermin, of course, soon set up home in the stacks and bred there in their larders, but they would be well and truly culled when threshing time came during the winter into spring. Dogs and boys then would have a field day striking them down and piling them up. Many boys like to fit in a few minutes 'mousing' before going to school, when the opportunity presented itself, and you could smell it on them when they entered the classroom. These great threshing engines, many of which were cut to pieces before today's steam enthusiasts could think about saving them, were superseded by tractors until the combine harvesters arrived, long after being introduced in America. Such threshing tackle as we see here is still used where the straw is needed for thatching. This is West's Farm again in 1931.

(District Library, Wisbech; Lilian Ream)

TYDD ST. GILES

This northernmost village in Cambridgeshire is six miles from Wisbech. Arriving from there, turning left past the church then right into Cat's Lane brings you alongside the Eau Dyke, where the scene today is as enchanting as it appears here in the early 1930s. Crossing the dyke by the Tretton bridge built in 1924 from funds provided jointly by the Ely and Holland District Councils, brings you immediately to the Lincolnshire boundary sign. The landscape here is early English with a wealth of fine trees with loud rookeries, broad grazing meadows and fine old houses. Lilian Ream has captured it with inspired simplicity, the dreaming period figure adding the perfect touch. The Eau Dyke was named after the wife of a 14th century Tydd landowner, its lower part being the Shire Drain, which was once an important boundary separating two counties, two dioceses and possibly two Anglo-Saxon kingdoms. It was superseded by the North Level Drain after 1834.

(District Library, Wisbech; Lilian Ream)

TYDD ST. GILES

Tydd church has a tower set well away from the main building, into which the bellringers climb to the first floor to sound their peals on three Sundays out of four, since the vicar administers three parishes. Nicholas Breakspear was the curate here in the 12th century. He became England's only pope, as Adrian the Fourth. The twin village of Tydd St. Mary, where the counties of Cambridgeshire, Norfolk and Lincolnshire meet, also had Breakspear as curate for a time. Fundraising to keep the church fabric in order has long been a part of village life and this was the scene at the annual church garden fete at Tydd St. Giles on Wednesday, June 1st, 1932, held in the tree-sheltered grounds adjoining the rectory at six in the evening. This is Eric Wilson and his band who played throughout the evening and at a dance later in the schoolroom, which continued until midnight. Eric became professor of music at Southampton University. Most of these villagers were sampling the new age of dance music before they had wireless in the homes. There were many such bands between the wars of varying standards. The two lads more intent on the photographer than the music are Albert Green in the cap, who became a milkman, and Neville Carter, a Tydd farmer born in a mud-and-osier marshland cottage, who now lives in a bungalow in the village.

(District Library, Wisbech; Lilian Ream)

6441   The Church, West Walton

WEST WALTON

Church towers built apart from the main building occur in Marshland, the reason being the need for suitable foundations. West Walton is two-and-a-half miles from Wisbech heading seawards and its isolated tower is a truly magnificent campanile, in size out of all proportion to all else in this small village. The main building is well buttressed following subsidence soon after it was built, so the search for better foundations for the campanile proved worthwhile. It is almost of cathedral proportions and it is a miracle there was money to spare for such wonderful structures in the 13th century. This view is from the 1920s.
(Wisbech and Fenland Museum; Henry Coates)

6442 Church Road, West Walton

WEST WALTON

Marshland may have found wealth in what was stolen from the sea but it remained for a long time at the sea's mercy and was catastrophically invaded by it in 1613, 1614 and 1670 and these disastrous years are commemorated in West Walton church. It is no surprise to find the other ancient monument in this parish to be the Roman bank raised to thwart the sea when it tried to recover its own. Close by the campanile stands the King of Hearts public house, seen here in the late 1920s when the tenant was Walter William Butcher. It is there still, not much altered apart from being smartened up for modern tastes. A secondary road leads to West Walton off the B198 from Wisbech, which enters the A47 to Lynn.

(Wisbech and Fenland Museum; Henry Coates)

WALPOLE HIGHWAY

Shot through by the busy A47 route to King's Lynn, the residents of this village must envy the rural peace enjoyed by its neighbours, Walpole St. Peter and Walpole St. Andrew. These saintly villages united in name in the heart of Marshland occur in clusters. This one has few architectural advantages. The church was built in the Norman style in 1844. In the 1850s the vicar of Walpole St. Peter, the Reverend Arthur Moore, who was also an artist in stained glass, created three windows for this church and commissioned four more from other artists. Although an amateur in the medium, Moore's qualities were recognised by the guardians of Ely cathedral and a fine example of his work is installed there, along with others of the period representing the Gothic revival. The glass from Walpole Highway has now been removed to Cambridge and the church is being converted into a private home. The village was formed out of several neighbouring parishes in 1933 and is big enough to maintain its school built in 1877, seen here in the 1930s with five of the boys equipped for long rides home. After leaving Walpole St. Peter the Reverend Arthur Moore became chaplain to Lord Melbourne.

(District Library, Wisbech; Lilian Ream)

TERRINGTON ST. JOHN

There are but two Terringtons, set well apart, and this one just over a mile along the A47 from Walpole Highway, catches most of the noise. For those who like traffic fumes on their country walks there is a well-kept footpath beside the A47 between these two assualted villages. The cottages in this view from the 1920s are still standing but the one on the left containing the bakery of Thomas Aitkin is now deserted, the lean-to replaced. Aitkin was succeeded here in the trade by Fred Kitchen. The post office in the middle was run by Horace and Hilda Rush and the garage on the right by Frederick Thomas Ward, who had taken over from Walter Bligh. Today the site just outside this picture on the right is occupied by J and I Motor Engineers. Two houses along to the left the baker today is Jonathan Rose. Here is another church, modest by Marshland standards, whose tower is more or less detached from the main structure. The difference here is that between tower and aisle there is a three-storied Priest's House intended to give overnight shelter, however discomfitting, to the priest travelling from Lynn or St. Clements, should the weather prevent his return.

(Wisbech and Fenland Museum; Henry Coates)

TERRINGTON ST. JOHN

It was quiet enough here when the sounds from the road came from horses and carts and farm implements. Then there was plenty of work for the farrier and blacksmith and this one in Terrington St. John is George High. He was a man of enterprise who began in neighbouring Tilney St. Lawrence and served as farrier in St. John for several years. While here he lived next to the garage in the previous picture. Later in life George became a bus driver after which he provided a delivery service and a small fleet of buses. George Clare, wheelwright and carpenter, worked nearby and this scene is outside the forge owned by his son Leslie. With George High here, holding the pony, is Ken Clare when St. John and St. Lawrence had many Clares and the time is the 1920s. Beyond the gate is the outbuilding belonging to the shop and post office also run by Horace Rush for a time. George High went back to Tilney St. Lawrence where he had a smallholding and an orchard, like many another hereabouts in the great days of Marshland fruit-growing.

(Dr. A. W. Greer Collection)

TILNEY ST. LAWRENCE.

TILNEY ST. LAWRENCE

Turning away from the traffic in St. John you enter the green acres of this pleasant, peaceful village. Yes, you may catch the sounds from the A47 when the wind is behind it, but only enough to remind you how lucky you are to be away from it. Lush meadows with trees aplenty abound here near this scene from the 1920s facing the crossroads leading left to Wiggenhall St. Mary Magdalen, right to St. John and straight on to the village school which is still open. On the right is the Buck Inn, also still open, where the landlord at this time was Thomas Griffin Drew. The buildings beyond it belong to Fairfield Farm, but they have gone now. The newsagent's shop on the corner where Walter Hewitt and later Mr. Whittel were in occupation is still open and run by K. Hall. The building behind it is part of the premises and the shop on the left had a succession of owners. H. Gathercole preceded J.A. Phillips who is the proprietor here. He was succeeded by E. Lack in 1939 who continued until 1969, after which the shop changed hands rapidly. The last to keep it open were Terry and Maureen Harness, but it closed in 1978 to become a private house.

(Dr. A.W. Greer Collection)

WALPOLE ST. PETER

Here we confront one of the two most splendid village churches in the land, long since referred to as The Queen of Marshland. A pleasant walk away from the A47, secure in its tranquillity, Walpole spawned the name that eventually gave England a prime minister. How in such a small village such a perpendicular masterpiece as this should have come to be built remains a mystery. When Sandringham became the Norfolk home of the Prince of Wales, who was to become Edward VII, and his bride Princess Alexandra, they discovered this church and made it their own. From that time it has received royal patronage and the visitors' book is full of royal signatures. When a maintenance fund was launched in 1931 the royal offerings for auction were as follows: HM the Queen — three framed pictures, including two watercolours; HM the Queen of Norway — a case of teaspoons; HRH the Duke of York (the future king) — a brass cigarette box. These were auctioned at the rectory garden fete on July 24th, 1931 raising £17—7s—0d, bringing the day's profits to £42—2s—3d. The aim was to raise £500, a huge sum then. The 15th century font here invites the visitor to 'Thynk and Thank', but thankfulness precedes thought in this place. This photograph is from the 1920s.
(Cambridgeshire Collection)

WALPOLE ST. PETER

This is a reminder that Walpole in all its Gothic glory was, like all Marshland villages, ever at the mercy of the sea from which the land was taken. These, however, are freshwater floods that occurred on September 5th and 6th, 1931. Many homes were flooded and this Wash Dyke area of Walpole was badly affected. The floods subsided very slowly and it was a long time before the land was workable again. Clearly the children here are loving it all, testing their wellies to the rim. February fill-dyke gave them ample opportunity to do this most years.

(District Library, Wisbech; Lilian Ream)

WALPOLE ST. ANDREW

A mile north of St. Peter, it was near this charming village that King John was supposed to have lost so much of his treasure, although relics of it have proved impossible to find. The king survived the loss, but not for long, his madness preceding his death. Excavations going as deep as thirty feet have yielded little more than the silt of the old seabed. Claims that the treasure was lost elsewhere remain unproven, but other sites have been chosen as more likely than St. Andrew. While its church can hardly be compared with that of its twin village, this 15th century example with its tower of red brick looks perfect in its setting as portrayed by Lilian Ream.

(District Library, Wisbech; Lilian Ream)

TERRINGTON ST. CLEMENT

This second masterpiece of Marshland is called the Cathedral of the Marshes and comparisons with that at Walpole would be odious. Four miles apart, the two churches taken together provide a moving experience. Terrington's coeval example was, nevertheless, never completed to the original design due to the prevalence of the Black Death. Many times it sheltered refugees from the invading sea. In 1607 supplies were boated from King's Lynn to sustain those hiding here, made homeless for a long time in this troublesome century for those on this reclaimed land. Here once more is a tower separate from the rest, this time at the side. The clock, as seen in this view from the 1920s, is still stuck at ten-past-three! The national school built in front of the church in 1861 did the view from the street no service, but the building now serves the continuing need for restoration funds.

(District Library, Wisbech; Lilian Ream)

Terrington Oddfellows Church Parade May 31st 1908

TERRINGTON ST. CLEMENT

This could be part of a town celebration, but it is that of a medium-sized Marshland village with a huge proportion of its population turning out for the Hospital Sunday parade. Led by the Long Sutton Town Band, the column is taking the long route to the church behind the trees which, for all its cathedral-like capacity, would be full for the special service. The late May weather is smiling, for those shades on the right are against the sun, not showers. The scene is instantly recognisable today, although I have no idea what today would bring so many people out on the street together. On the left is the grocery long kept by Walter Webb with the post office next door behind the lamppost. Next is the King William public house, still open, and on this day expecting a lively trade later on. The shop became a sweetshop, another grocery, a carpet shop and finally a shoemaker's shop and a centre for key-cutting, closing down in 1991. The Independent Order of Oddfellows were behind this parade and another later on arranged for the Methodists.

(Central Divisional Library, King's Lynn)

Magdalen Bridge Norfolk No.

WIGGENHALL ST. MARY MAGDALEN

Magdalen is threequarters-of-a-mile from the station on the London — King's Lynn line formerly known as Magdalen Road but now named Watlington, the village adjacent. Magdalen had 761 inhabitants in 1911 just before this photograph was taken. On the west side of the Great Ouse, this bridge to it was in a state of dereliction and was soon to be replaced by one suitable for modern traffic and this is now due to be replaced to serve present needs. Meadows and remaining orchards add charm to this little village. The ancient glass in the north aisle of its 15th century church depicts more than forty saints. Crabb's Abbey is an old farmhouse where once lived nuns in the perfect peace they sought. Of the four Wiggenhalls, that of St. Mary the Virgin beyond the Middle Level Drain five miles from Lynn has a church now redundant but well preserved and it is supposed to be haunted. It contains a tomb of the Kerville family once of these parts. This family founded St. Mary's Hall here in the reign of Henry VII. A tiny community, St. Mary the Virgin is one-and-a-half miles from Wiggenhall St. Germans on the other side of the Ouse.

(Dr. A.W. Greer Collection)

WIGGENHALL ST. GERMANS

If this village is no great tourist attraction today these cherishable pictures show that it might have been. This is a view of one half of The Square in its centre and most of this part remains. That immediately behind the wagon has been replaced but modern ideals of maintenance, modern excrescences, not to mention parked cars, have banished enchantment. The postman behind stands near the Black Horse public house which was also shop and post office. Another house with shop stands there today. Landlord of the Black Horse was Frederick J. Bales. The large house on the right remains but shorn of its green cover and the house on the left is still there too. This photograph dates from after the First World War.

(Central Divisional Library, King's Lynn)

101

The Square, Wiggenhall St. Germans. (*Samson's Series.*) J 2121.

WIGGENHALL ST. GERMANS

The tall house here is the one on the right in the preceding photograph and it later became The Chequers public house where mine host was Moffin Andrews. The shop is better seen here — and better still later with the creeper removed, revealing the proprietor's name, A.E. Bushell. The charming row of cottages has been swept away and replaced by ugly commercial buildings. On the extreme right lived Cyril Brooks, cycle dealer. Without the presence of the van this scene might as convincingly date from the turn of the century, but it has to be much later. The bakers were William James Bear and Son of 69 and 71 Friar's Street, South Lynn, who were also millers. Unquestionably the little girl near the van would be savouring the aroma of new crust and badly wanting a slice with butter while the baker may well have been enjoying a cup of tea inside. Suddenly the five miles from Lynn to Wiggenhall St. Germans became as nothing to such travelling vendors. From this time they could cover a lot of miles in a week, get home betimes and put the ponies out to pasture or up for sale.

(Central Divisional Library, King's Lynn)

WIGGENHALL ST. GERMANS

Nearby at the head of the Middle Level Drain is the great sluice and pumping station of St. Germans, indispensable to the drainage of the fens. When powered by steam the pumps could lift 3,000 tons of water a minute. The sluice collapsed in the 1880s but it was repaired and the mended cracks stood out for years. Wiggenhall St. Germans is seven miles from The Wash and this bridge over the widening Ouse received extensive repairs in 1911 just after this photograph was taken. At this time the tollman here was Tom Page. The stone and concrete bridge that replaced it took little account of the view made beautiful by the church.

(Central Divisional Library, King's Lynn)

WIGGENHALL ST. GERMANS

The Reverend Alfred Legge MA had been vicar of this parish for forty-three years when this photograph was taken in 1914. The curate at Wiggenhall St. Peter, half-a-mile downstream, was the Reverend Maurice Barnard George. The two parishes were united in 1892 and in 1918 the Reverend George was made vicar of Guyhirn, leaving the church of St. Peter to become derelict. His daughter, Margaret, became a dedicated photographer. These carol singers were trained by the Reverend and Mrs. George and for several nights coming up to the Christmas of 1914 they sang their way round the linked parishes to raise money for the Church of England Homes for Waifs and Strays. Leading them were the George sisters, Margaret and Emeline, third and fourth from the left of the back five in this group. Few signs of the war show on these happy faces. The boys were not old enough to qualify for call-up during the next four tragic years, but they may well have been caught up in the next World War. As an instance, the population of St. Peter in 1911 was 269 and this went down to 216 due to the demands of the 1914—18 War.

(Central Divisional Library, King's Lynn)

CONTENTS

FEN and MARSHLAN VILLAGES

A Portrait in Old Photographs and Picture Postcards

by

Anthony Day

S. B. Publications